Live
Lose
Learn

A poetry Collection

Live
Lose
Learn

A poetry Collection

Mari Howard

HODGE PUBLISHING

Copyright © 2019 Clare M Howard Weiner writing as Mari Howard.

Published by Hodge Publishing,
10 Bainton Road, Oxford, OX2 7AF

ISBN 978-0-9564769-8-2

British Library Cataloguing in Publication Data.

A catalogue record for this book is available
from the British Library.

Cover design and typesetting:
Rachel Lawston, Lawston Design

1.

Family...
growing baby, child,
and onwards towards
old age...

Life is Becoming

Life is becoming...
We stand on unsteady feet
clutching the furniture,
staring,
transfixed,
into the wonderland beyond –

Or, *trans-fixed*,
Crucified upon necessity.
Pinned down, pinned *out*,
like butterflies,
at a closed door...

Life is becoming,
As, becoming in our outfits,
we steal into Wonderland,
drop disguises,
seize a jazz trumpet
and discover playing our tune –

Who, though, will un-pin those tattered,
clipped-winged
butterflies?
Dis-entomb the crucified,
Warm the buds frosted in May,
Love up muted hues till colours sing?

Life is becoming when we nurture nature...

Prism

My grandfather's prisms, kept on his study windowsill, became my introduction to science

I hold a prism in my palm –
many-faceted jewel, carefully cut,
which, in its turn,
cuts and spreads light.
Rainbows. Promises.

Move on? Transfigure?

I take another look:
each face, scratched, etched,
patterned, written,
allowed to be.

Childhood cuts unruly patterns,
adolescence is for experiments,
adult slowly carves
maturity.

If I drop this prism
into forgetting's pond,
then, obeying nature,
its rings would widen out, concentric.

Itself plummeting the while
into all-embracing mud,
blind, lost.

I pocket it:
The future may review its memory-bank or chip.

Crystal storage. Life's geology. Rainbows.

Love Medicine/Crones

*A young woman poet came to read
at our writing group . . .*

She bounced: love was new,
skilled,
untried, and
just invented (especially for her)...

I, a crone in velvet,
lurked among the shadows.

She described the scan –
painless,
high-tech,
as scenery... mystic, wonderful...

I saw Arthur's sword
pierce my heart –
and Lucifer's pierce
Mary Virgin's at the Cross.

This woman shrank back,
glossed over birth, the blood
and pain between love and
the beloved's cries...

Oh pretty, pretty world of childhood...
crowned with thorns,
white organza party-dresses
stained purple-blue
with crushed, acerbic juice
of black-currants...

the black currents of our lives...
precious love
poignant tears
heart-holds... and lettings-go...

'til we become crones,
crones in velvet.

The Visit

*My friend described returning to the old family home:
her memories were romantic, tinged with distaste*

I remember, I remember,
the house where I was born...

a damp autumn,
apple-fall time,
the wasps buzz around the plums,
within and without...

Here's the crazy-paved path
I walked as a child
and under my feet the sandy, refined
earth of an ants'-nest,

and foot-trodden pears.
The door's ajar – is this the house
of my womb-nurture,
where I sucked milk of human

kindness, and learned
at mama's knee? French knitting,
the alphabet, and God?
Paint's blistered in the sun.

No matter... I enter the darkness,
the table laid for one,
and that, a fly,
beating on the window.

The catch hangs loose
putty falls from the frame
like stale crusts.
The glass, opaque, balanced precarious.

'Mother!'
I call –

The house shifts a little,
decay clutches my throat with its
dry and leathered claw
I retch out love...
wishing
there were hugs and tears...

Mothering Sunday

Written as a mum of young adults...
It can take that to understand valuing your mum!

Mother, I miss you
more now
that I grow old...

That I see my hands
as if gloved in your
roughened skin,
pleated by the years...

That I find myself
taking down, again,
sugar, flour, baking tins,
and see us Russian dolls –

three generations –
you, me, and she I carried
womb-safely, each cake-makers... passionate women,
fierce with love...

Mama, my garden's planted for you –
scarlet-eyed polyanthus,
roses, everything...
but especially
the polys –

my favourite,
baby-flowers,
first-remembered
colour... eyes of
first-warm spring...

I need you, mama, now!
Over the warm smoothness
of the ironing board – that
fresh-boiled scent, the sunbeams...

I weep – that Sunday-evening peace...
your less-fulfilled,
and choice-free life,
the schoolmarm tones,
not lost –

I miss being not me but
Like a class of twenty but
I was one, alone... missed hugs and cuddles –

miss your non-existent grave,
where flowers have no place to be –

reach up my worn-glove hands
to meet yours,
leaned down from that heaven
you conjured up, so

we can touch – now, mama, now –
that I know your
daughter-inflicted
pain –
to console your
mama's heart…

and kiss you,
tender with better, understanding,
love.

The X-wives

Today I'm thinking about the x-wives –
tomorrow and yesterday I will write
or wrote
otherwise,
but today, it is the x-wives.

Our town is full of them,
Like autumn leaves, colourful, fragile, they float
Freely, or fall in a reign of tears
To become slippery underfoot,
something stuck to someone else's shoes.

Our town is full of them: why, only in one week I heard
Of two philosophers who dropped a wife,
Careless of what she meant or was meant to mean,
Whether she was culturally relevant or
Passé in extreme.

X-wives have the x-factor to x-treme,
And are neither x-ceptionally clever nor beautiful,
These are x-perimental wives, who bear the first child,
And hold your hand at the first mortgage application...

... trophies are for later ... shields,
or silvered chalices ...
shiny and svelte,
Ready to bear the second batch of sprogs...

After Halloween comes...

All Saints' & All Souls' Tide

'The Commemoration of All Faithful Departed'

'Time like an ever-rolling stream
Bears all its sons away
They fly forgotten as a dream
Flies at the break of day.'

Time, like an ever-rolling stream ... or
like waves, breaking on the shore,
pulls at each withdrawal
some mass of pebbles,
indifferently makes choices to bear away
and smooth,
dumping them elsewhere on the beach ...

I see them, each a soul ...

A soul within a context:
The antique desk, a candle, fine china,
a prayer. . . the one whom All Saints' Tide
this year bore away ...
And another – sixty years her junior, un-timely,
who dyed our bath deep purple,
whom I'd admonished for leaving a trail
of peach-stones, and sticky doorknobs,
in our house –

A favourite Uncle, who mirrored a father gone –

My unassuming friend,
beloved of special-needs children,
crushed, by a bus ...

My father, defying medical advice,
hastening uphill,
to buy real farmhouse cheddar (with a rind) ...

My aunt – the star pupil, unfulfilling early promise,
breathed her last in poverty, and her sister's arms –

My mother wondered if her life –
based on ideas of service
– had made a difference –
and supposed the old attic-bedroom wardrobe
of her childhood
haunted her hospital room –

Time's waves reared up and took them all,
relentless breakers, sifting, plashing, pounding
    and re-shaping
our own lives, left behind.

Memory, an echo in a shell, held to our ears
mimics untouchable realities which once
defined us.

I light a candle,
Un-forgetting, determining
eternity must not be a dream,
and that All Souls' Day is a feast in heaven.

When the matriarch
mother-in-law departs ...

I Shall Not Forget

I shall not forget seeing
you,
hands stilled,
perfect nails, fluttering fingers, now
set fast, clutching air –

I shall not forget you
curled unmovable
in your second birthing blanket
foetus to foetus after ninety years.

I shall not forget how ordinary
extraordinary you became,
passed through that
universal door, unable to
will yourself a different journey –

the struggle had been between
invincibility
and love
but, till now,
you did not understand…

Pixels

The photo on the service-sheet

Your eyes – bright with promise –
Your lips – parted in a laugh –
Your elegant hands, supple,
able,
playful –

The world's your oyster, and
no doubt,
oysters were bought for you –
more than once…

It's all there in the picture,
gaiety,
the future…

But it's all pixels, pixie –
Little dots of black and white –
It cannot be you
for you are flesh, and spirit,

actions, not
dotted shadows
shot in a second,
burned on the page...

... yet we are all marked,
patterned over,
with your stamp,
mother...

After the Funeral

After the funeral, several
Things took place...

Something flew
heavenwards, satisfied
we had done justly;

Weights fell
from our necks,
so seeing the sky became again
a possibility;

Silence stirred – like a blessing –
and... there was laughter.

After the funeral,
finality became a beginning...

Sisters ... Crossing the Road

Two 80-year olds, one widowed, one never married ...

I see them coming,
eager to meet him
chaliced in silver
hidden in bread.
Like birds – like wrens –
one blue, one brown,
clasping hands, sisters always,
are crossing the road.

One leads the other,
for safety,
hoops for bowling –
sticks for walking –
it is all the same.

And now atop the sheets
hands are clasped
for crossing in safety
into his arms –
no longer chaliced
or hidden,
but open-armed –
perhaps as Mother waited
for girls on an errand
when the last century
was young.

Life like a journey
carried them far,
but now, like singing birds,
like angels unaware,
sisters, together,
are crossing the road.

2.

Goodbye...
Cutting the ties that
try to bind...

Suddenly October

Suddenly, October.
It came overnight – as months do, you know,
creeping up behind the moonlight
to flip the calendar over and show
a different picture.

Suddenly, October,
I see you in winter's light
lizard-eyed, half-listening, half
God knows where.
You, the naughtiest boy in the Sunday School
grown middle-aged,
and wonder what it was you did
to drive that innocent lady, probably a spinster,
to distraction.

Your mischievous eyes
fix me with a quizzical look,
then turn away.
Suddenly, October.

Warm thoughts
in past years
melted the glacier
which was my heart…
but always you have measured my tears in a glass,
and your words, like fiery spirits
on the rocks.
Suddenly, October, and the wind blows cold.

Writing Exercise

At a poetry-group workshop

She said:
*Think of an object,
its associations,
the daily life of its wearer –*

She chose *her mother's apron* – as
the image of your tie, a friendly serpent
gazing like the seraphim with all its paisley eyes
came to me
un-bid.

(I'd learned, under-five,
this habit – looking people in the chest,
faces being too exalted.)

I mused upon those serpentine eyes: ever-open,
do they now gaze,
clinically of course,
upon the inside of a wardrobe,
a wooden drawer,
the silken lining of a pocket
in the last suit you wore?

Those multifarious eyes may now close, be still,
no more sharing of your daily life,
the snake untangle from the pole,
Moses lay down his staff,
symbolic serpent slither off,
across the sand. Aesculapius sleeps,
silken skin sloughed off,
and body-prints in shifting sand
are blown by winds of time –

Just as I thought these things,
so she recalled
her mother's apron –

Queen of the fair

On the Front at St Ives

The carousel
stops: but its giddy whirling
still sickens me. A searing sun
beats on the fairground.
Hot-dog vans reeking of onions,
sweet illusive candy-floss,
and melting ice-creams,
add to the nauseous soup
of memory.

Pain pulses in the fluorescent colours
of buckets and spades, displayed
in little, ancient, shop-fronts,
opened out to sell to tourists.
I want this sand, coloured like golden
caster sugar,
flat like it's been steam-rollered
by action of the sea,
to be a meeting-place for you and me.

That's not right: I want
to catch the moment, reproduce the song
your voice sang
in my left ventricular vena cava –
in other words, half the seat
of my emotions –
the other half responded
without thought,
a song for you.

But a song too loud,
fluorescent, like those
buckets and spades, pink swirly-patterned,
plastic,
in-your-face,
a fairground woman, riding a painted horse,
whirling,
like her thoughts.

Let's try again, urges the pain,
let's try among white-painted walls,
cool fountains of living water,
a bench beneath a vine,
a glass of wine.

Tell me when your life might end...

Parting laid a lily between us
– a lily of *annunciation*...

When we talk now,
it is around this flower,
this representative of
virginity, death,
and resurrection...

this soft, white, curled-around trumpet
of petal-cells,
designed by God to represent
purity.

And, when we expect to die –
you, or I,
we'll have to send the other one a white lily –
"MI expected, noon on Sunday...
last breath due, Thursday night. . ."
Or some-such.

See you in church, the message might run,
I shall not expect a wreath...

I will be the lady in a velvet-spotted veil,
by the wicket-gate... you, the gentleman
who someone thought was seated at the back...
who seems to have
slipped away...

who declined
sherry and fruitcake...
who had to catch a train...
who offered lilies to his Magdalene...

3.

And the wryly humorous business of picking oneself up... and *moving on*...

Unstick

Unstick the Elastoplast
fast
one pull should do it –
off the wound!

Mum says
the pain is less
this way...

all through
childhood,
we practised...

but when the wound was in
our hearts
what then?

women wax their legs
go through the sharp
hot ripping
pain

men are less brave

women are forced to push the pain
out, and away,
upon the birthing-day
as Mum knew...

men, proprietorial and blasé,
know not the wound

they are the Elastoplast,
sticky, fragrant, pink –

don't think the dirt won't stick
the corners fold back,
flap,
scruff the knees of tomboy girls
resilient, tough as trees... you got that wrong!

Paying such late attention to the wound
won't help it heal – *I pick the scab, you say...*

But such heart wounds require
more than what men desire.

You turn your back,
cover your ears, and rip...

and now your hand could dip
inside my heart, and feel its drumming beat...

A Woman without a Man

From the feminist phrase (of disputed origin)
'A woman without a man is like a fish without a bicycle'

A woman without a man is
worse off than
a fish without a bicycle...
a fish can swim,
but a woman cannot slim...

I lost a man and I gained
two stone in weight... 'cos I'd gone straight to
incense,
bath-bombs,
hot water bottles in bed,
hot-buttered toast (*with* honey),
seconds of everything,
sugaring my black coffee,
bourbon biscuits by threes,
hot choc every night,
and chocolate eaten in the street....

Soooo, soon I was buying clothes (with zips that met),
elastic-waisted trousers,
CDs to drown my sorrows,
alcohol to drown the CDs,
counselling,
new friends to replace ones I'd worn through, like hankies
    with tears...

All this added up,
this larval being wore
*XL trousers when once I'd been
a size-12 sylph.*
Then...the larva split,
... released my butterfly soul
... I understood the feeling...
... What was left?

The larval skin, still suffering
heartburn,
and heartache,
reached for the fruit-bowl,
for pears (like pairs)
are sweet...

Oh, for God's sake! *Give this fish-woman
a bicycle for Christmas!*
An exercise bike.
Learn that *a woman with a bicycle*
is better off than *a fish with a man*...

Country-style love

Time for some nonsense!

Got a song about a real sweet guy
thinks that grin and wave he's got will make gals die
thinks I didn't wanna be a dame
thinks that love and care's a game –
brother, *it's not over until the fat lady sings.*

Youthful innocent with eyes of blue
didn't think I'd go and fall for you –
played you were a little bit naive
thought you'd be Adam and I'd play Eve –
So where were you when they made the apes,
don't you know about their japes?
I said *it's not over until the fat lady sings!*

Well now with you so come-on tricksy
I don't have to dress up itsy-bitsy,
spider calls me up his web
he's a smoothie and not a pleb
put his hands inside my heart
turns around, calls me the tart!
Oh no, *it's not over until the fat lady sings!*

... think I'm gonna get my surgeon's knife,
try applying that to your life ...
see how you like it with the boot
on the other foot and oh dear, shoot!
your picture's on the front page at last
seduction, lies, your reputation's past –
I said *it's not over until the fat lady sings!*

Now ...

Now the wound is healed,
the scar has become a sort of
friend ...

Now, when you've drained away,
like pus from a boil,
you still remain ...

Now you will be for a while
or maybe for ever
the extra chromosome that
gives my mind dysmorphic features.

Or the footprint of that virus that
never quite leaves the body
having incorporated itself,
its damn great
footprint,
into my DNA

And I shall never be quite so
alone
again ...

A Parting Gift

Over, and the learning...

Thank you for parting,

Thank you for making it
curtains for me –

Unthinkingly you drew aside an obstacle
which was occluding the light
engineered the dawn,
let particles
come together,
neurons communicate
electricity send messages
once again...
or rather, for the first time...

You snatched scales away with stealthy scalpel
when your time was ripe,
made what was partly visible
more clear,
polished the glass through which we see
but darkly. . .

Set innocence to rest,
gave serpent-knowledge to my virgin
soul,
handed over the tools for life
from behind the veil,
as you took your bow
behind the safety curtain.

4.

It wasn't
much different...

Being a woman
2000 years ago

Christmas:

Mary considers the Wise Men's Gifts

The Star was beautiful: imagine,
God set a new jewel in the heavens,
Another window...
Another sparkling eye looked down,
Another guardian beacon blazed on high...

But, the gifts... disturbing, over the top,
Not rejected – no – but, *not quite us, you know*...
The gifts gazed back at me, from their corner,
The gold discomforted amongst our earthen vessels –
The sweet and the bitter scents,
The resin and the herbs,
Incense of worship,
Myrrh of mourning –
Seeping from their intricately carved and decorated boxes
... Like I say, *too much*...

I looked again at the Child in my arms – he reached
Towards the costly things, as babies do,
Hands like flowers, open, accepting them.

The golden thurible, being rather too grand for our house,
But the child insistent,
I carefully took coals from the bread oven,
And incense from its box,
And using an earthenware dish,
Clouded the house with smoke...

It was like a sacrifice, really –
    I can't say I warmed to it...
        My other children have
        been easier to understand...

Epiphany

The Magus's Wife's Tale

Sophia responds to T. S. Eliot's Journey of the Magi

I doubt not he's returned depressed – him and the other
    two, disappointed,
with no armies to support,
empire to negotiate with,
encouragement in – polishing up this world
till it shines with wisdom
like that star glitters in the universe,
announcing its proud, planetary presence –

PROGRESS, *modernity*, and *moving on!*

Wisdom?

Huh – What can I say?

We *are* the Silken Girls, with the sherbet –
and they – the Wise Ones – they see *only that* –
Sherbet with arms –
(and legs and breasts of course) –
sherbet with dancing veils,
gyratory bellies,
jewelled and scented –

Satisfactory?

I should like to see *them* satisfied!

Would think a baby in the straw more
    like a *puzzle* to them,
than *satisfaction* –
and a dubious satisfaction it seems,
judging by the tone of it –

Birth – and death – I shake my head at this *profundity*,
– linked them up,
he did, tumbled to it at last!
– and my jewelled headdress rings –
how close they come to truth for once,

hard and bitter agony he says
– he who has not laboured to give birth and
knows not the connections –

So – we disguised ourselves – me, her, and
the other one – just the three of us girls –
travelled as boys, in the pantomime tradition
    of the season –

solstice over, we enjoyed the better weather,
happier camels
without the snow –

just as well seeing we had further to travel,
all the way to Egypt –

And I must say I *was* impressed –
the world turned upside down, I'd say,
and him set to do it again, that baby –

The clue to wisdom is an open mind, and
a bit of respect for strange happenings –

And Wisdom – didn't I read somewhere
she *is a woman?*

Hadn't my own wealth to buy anything impressive,
but, being somehow disillusioned
with serving sherbet to grouchy old men with telescopes
and astral charts
I offered what I do have

a heart and a pair of hands –
suggested they could do with a nanny for the child

– this way, *I can watch what becomes of him* –
be *there* when he comes into his kingdom –

(you never know, do you,
what the future might hold?)

Maybe he is a king,
some kind of king or
a god or a hero?

A Pot of Ointment

The sex-worker's Story...

This aromatic ointment,
– nard or valerian, Eastern visitor –
roll the words around your tongue
pause to appreciate
sensuality,
and scent,
picture the bazaar,
dust and sweat,
donkey dung,
musky camels, sour milk
– the day he purchased it...

he had been a Roman,
greasy, fat...

what with everything –
the baby crying as he had his will,
the other children, sent out to play
and keep ignorance of a widow's managing –

– what with that, and her
sore and beaten body
broken for her brood,
she'd tripped on the threshold,
dropped the pot.

Fragrance everywhere:
despair,
humiliation,
and all those eyes,
each pair
male, and aware...
salivating even as they
roundly criticised...

She wept... and then, having no cloth to hand,
dried him with her hair...
so things went from
bad to worse,
in there...

The Roman guy returned –
angry she'd thrown away his gift –
said 'See where your lover's ended up,'
and pointed to the hill...
then tucked more spices inside her bodice, yet...

she couldn't keep the myrrh and incense
... eve of the Passover,
she watched them take the bodies down...
noted the grave...

Broken like my earthen vessel,
she understood,
and all that fragrance of his life,
his love,
his careful insights,
poured out
for dry and dusty earth to drink...

And at that first-available dawn,
poised to anoint him –
this time from intention –
she understood...

No, not the tender of the garden,
I AM *he you sought* –

healing takes place, as it ought,
not by return to past lives but
with transformation...

Those leering eyes,
re-formulating what she did,
wrote up
an alabaster pot . . .

and named her as a prophet of his
sacrifice,
and one who understood
inevitable as
intention,
and the pricelessness
of an itinerant preacher, and a woman of the night...

Easter

Don't Touch

Being Mary

First she had to get to know herself
without the demons. Moved by his love
they'd fled
and she came
cleanly and coolly forward with the ointment
not for his head but for his feet –
yet feet are a symbol of sexuality.
Intimate feet, vulnerable, bony,
closest to the earth
full of energy
and liveliness.
His feet were hardened by walking,
strong, bronzed by the sun and the soles
were thick with five layers of skin
and his sandals were old and mended
many times.
Lightly she took each foot
in turn
in her hands
removed the shoe
and wept over it, the foot which
marched all over Judea, taking the tidings of peace, and
would never be passed down the generations
as a characteristic of her babies.

She let down her hair,
so that it flowed

over her shoulders, thick and black
with little red highlights.
Tears gathered in her eyes when she remembered
taking down her hair for her clients
when all she wanted
was him.

She poured the ointment on his feet
and heard Judas mithering about money again.

The Pharisees, seeing the eroticism of it all
curled their lips in disapproval.

He let her do it.

But in the garden,
embracing times were over.
'Don't touch,' he said,
warning her of breaking the spell
of resurrection.

Maybe she,
womanly, humanly loving,
warm, soft, and morning-fresh,
was just what he wanted
just then
and that was the very last, the last temptation.

A mother's memories

*Another Mary recalls the 'Wise Men' who visited,
and has some joined-up insights*

Magi – *wise men?*
Odd, the gifts they brought. Gold we couldn't make a use of,
A family like ours, artisans, respectable of course...
Sell it? Where'd we have obtained that sort of thing, they'd
    ask, (inferring reception of goods no doubt
obtained in some less than honest way...)
    Expensive spices?

No... I kept them, though,
Wrapped in a carpet rather too good to use on
    ordinary occasions,
Wedding present from my cousin, Elizabeth,
    and Zechariah,
Older parents – whose boy was, himself, rather odd...
    a visionary...

When we go up to the Feast – Passover, I mean – We have
    to take them along with us, those *gifts*,
Can't have someone see them in the house, or in the
    workshop,
What'd be said?

So... as I was saying, about to tell you... I came back
    that day,
Black it was, the sun veiled, the clouds tearing their clothes,

And took a look at them, the gifts for a king. . .
Saw it again, the spear in his side, shuddering, and
    remembered Simeon –
A sword will pierce your heart as well. . .

Yes . . .

And wrapped them up again, quick,
Except for the myrrh – which I gave to Mary Magdalene –
She's a good girl, caring, unafraid, she'd take it to the tomb
Come the morning. . .

Well, back she came, Mary, laughing,
crying, laughing… the golden sun illuminating her tears –
I saw him,
we talked,
in the garden…

Magi?
Wise men?
I suppose it's possible. . .